My Heavenly Father's
HEART

My Heavenly Father's
HEART
POEMS

Written by

CORINNE MCCOY

ARPress
ILLUMINATING IDEAS.
EMPOWERING VOICES

ARPress
45 Dan Road Suite 5
Canton MA 02021

Hotline: 1(888) 821-0229
Fax: 1(508) 545-7580

Ordering Information:
Quantity sales. Special discounts are available on quantity purchases by corporations, associations, and others. For details, contact the publisher at the address above.

Printed in the United States of America.

ISBN-13:	Softcover	979-8-89389-979-5
	Hardcover	979-8-89389-980-1
	eBook	979-8-89389-978-8

Library of Congress Control Number: 2024918678

Acknowledgments

To my Heavenly Father - Thank You for putting the words in my heart to write these poems.

Mr. Roy Austin, my 8th grade teacher who encouraged me to keep writing poems. Without his encouragement, this book would not have been written.

I thank my friends who knew about the book have prayed and encouraged me while I was writing.

My Father who taught me about God. My Father lived what he taught. He lived his faith, trust, and love for God in his everyday life.

Here are some notes from a couple lessons my Father taught and a poem I have written about my Father.

First Note:

Faith will still find scope in the ever deepening mysteries of the unfathomable wisdom of God, and hope will still look onward to some fresh fulfillment of God's purpose, but love is the very greatest, for it is of the very character of God.

Second Note:

Jesus is the truth about God. He is more than just a teacher. He is complete and absolute. Finally, the Lord told His disciples that they need not fear for they have His peace.

Do not be troubled, Christ is the way to successful service for God. He is the way to answered prayer. He gives the Holy Spirit to comfort and guide. We do not have to be worried about his absence; He has promised that He will come again.

My Father

I never heard my Father say,
"I love you;" instead, he showed me;
He showed me God's love as well.

My Father taught me to work our ranch;
Taught me to till, plant, and water the ground;
And he taught me when to harvest.

My Father taught me to care for cattle;
To train and ride horses;
He taught me to play games.

While I was little,
My Father held me on his lap
As he studied God's Word.

My Father taught me that
Jesus is the Truth about God,
And Love is the very character of God.

My Father showed me God's love,
By helping other people in need;
My Father lived the life he taught;
He was always there for me.

Foreword

These poems have been written to encourage and strengthen people in their daily walk with God; and to bring glory and honor to Him.

The poems speak of creation to Jesus birth, death, and resurrection to His second coming and the end of this world. They speak of the new heaven and new earth to come.

When we feel alone, afraid, or are in trouble, we can go to our Heavenly Father. He will always be there for us no matter where we are in life. God will be with us in the good times as well as helping us through the bad or time of trouble. All we need to do is reach out and ask Him for His help.

May God bless you as you read the poems.

My Heavenly Father's Heart

My Heavenly Father loves us so much
That His Son He sent as a baby
Born in a stable, in a manger was laid.

To shepherds, angels proclaimed Jesus birth.
Gifts of gold, frankincense, and myrrh,
Brought by Wisemen following a star.

In wisdom and stature Jesus did grow;
By John, He was baptized,
His Heavenly Father was well pleased.

Into the wilderness Jesus went,
By Satan He was tempted,
With scripture, Jesus rebuked him.

Jesus began His ministry
Teaching in parables,
Showing kindness, love, and compassion.

Jesus forgave many of their sins,
He healed the sick, lame, and paralyzed;
Demons, He cast out and raised people from death.

The blind saw and the deaf heard.
With a young boy's lunch,
Jesus fed thousands of people.

In the midst of storm on the sea,
Jesus spoke the wind and waves obeyed;
In your storms of life, peace He will give.

Religious authorities became jealous;
Jesus, they did plot to kill.
An arrest and trials took place.

On a cross, Jesus was crucified,
He cried, "It is finished!" and died;
On the first day of the week, He arose.

In love, my Heavenly Father gave
His only Son to redeem all
Who believe and accept Him in their hearts.

My Heavenly Father knows our thoughts;
He knows when we are hurting;
He knows whether we are sad or happy.

O friend, my Jesus loves you,
And wants you, your heart to Him bring.
Will you give Jesus your heart, your life?

For to you, healing, peace, and love
The Father will give.
This is my Heavenly Father's heart of love.

God's Creation

With love God created the heavens and earth.
Waters and mountains He put in their place;
Trees, flowers, and plants in their place.
The animals and sea creatures He also created.

Over and around rocks and corners
The waters sing and dance, praising God.
The mountains stand majestically as
Earth's alters unto God.

A gentle breeze plays music through
Trees, flowers, and plants
In reverence, praise, and honor,
All the animals bow their heads to God.

With love God created man in His own image;
He created woman from man's side;
Not to walk in front, nor behind,
But by his side as a helpmate.

In six days, God created everything.
"It is good," He said and rested the seventh day.
God blessed and sanctified the seventh day;
In love He gave it to us to rest and worship Him;
To remember His creation and His love for us.

Written by Corinne McCoy

Crystals From The Sky

Rain was sent down
From clouds above
To water the earth
To keep it cool and moist.

Rain was sent from above
That trees and flowers
May grow strong and beautiful
 For all to see their splendor.

Rain was sent from above
To fill the lakes, rivers, streams, and oceans
 For fish and other creatures to live in;
And for animals to drink and bathe in.

Rain was sent from above;
One day, as it fell
Each drop sparkled in the sun –
Sparkled like soft crystals.

These crystals glittered and danced
With beauty and grace as they fell.
Beauty and Grace only God can create;
These crystals from the sky.

Keep My Commandments

Keep My commandments, My child,
They are My covenant with you.
If you love Me, keep them all,
And all will be well with you.

If you love Me, My child,
Keep My commandments, and
I will ask My Father in heaven
To send the Spirit to guide you.

If you love Me, My child,
Obey all of My commandments,
And the Holy Spirit will guide you
Into all truth and understanding.

If you love Me, My child,
The Holy Spirit will teach you
To live, to love, to forgive as I have.
If you love Me, keep My commandments.

John 14:15

If you love me, you will keep
My commandments.

Exodus 20:2-7

"I am the Lord your God, who brought you out of the land of Egypt, out of the house of bondage. "You shall have no other gods before me. "You shall not make for yourself a graven image, or any likeness of anything that is in heaven above, or that is in the earth beneath, or that is in the water under the earth; you shall not bow down to them or serve them; for I the Lord your God am a jealous God, visiting the iniquity of the Fathers upon the children to the third and fourth generation who hate me, but showing steadfast love to thousands of those who love Me and keep My commandments. "You shall not take the name of the Lord you God in vain; for the Lord will not hold him guiltless who takes His name in vain.

God First

God created heaven and earth
And everything in them;
You and me; He created.

Put God first in your hearts;
He will guide you all your days;
Wondrous works in you He will do.

Put God first in your life;
He desires our devotion to Him;
Our desires He will fill.

Turn away from idols;
Nothing will they do;
They only sit in blank stare.

Put God first in your minds;
He desires our worship;
Worship Him in all you do.

God loves us,
He is true and just;
Put God first in all things.

Remember The Sabbath

God has given us a day of rest,
A day to remember all He has done,
A day to worship Him.

In six days God created the earth
And all that is in and above it;
 On the seventh day He rested.

God commanded us to rest,
And keep the seventh day holy;
He called the seventh day Sabbath.

"Remember the Sabbath day,
To keep it holy," He said;
This is God's holy day for us.

Remember the beauty of God's creation;
Remember the blessings He has given us;
Remember the love He has shown us.

Remember to give all glory to God;
Remember to worship and praise God;
Remember the Sabbath day, keep it holy.

Exodus 20:8-11

"Remember the Sabbath day, to keep it holy. Six days shall you labor and do all your work; but the seventh day is a Sabbath to the Lord your God; in it you shall not do any work, you, or your son, or your daughter, or your man servant, or your maid servant, or your cattle, or the sojourner who is within your gates; for in six days the Lord made heaven and earth, the sea, and all that is in them, and rested the seventh day; therefore the Lord blessed the Sabbath day and hallowed it.

Exodus 20:12

Honor your Father and your Mother,
that your days may be long in the land
which the Lord your God gives you.

Written by Corinne McCoy

Honor Your Parents

Honor your Father and Mother;
Listen to your parents;
They were your age once.

Give honor to your Parents;
Obey them willingly
And God will bless you.

Honor your Father;
He gives you guidance
Throughout your life.

Honor your Mother;
She cares and nurtures you;
She loves and prays for you always.

God is honored and blessed
When you listen and obey
And give honor to your Parents.

My Master's Touch

I watched birds flying and realize,
My Master touched their wings
To give them flight.

I see the trees, flowers, and bushes;
And see my Master touch them;
And they grow strong and beautiful.

A heart was broken and deeply hurting;
My Master said, "Come to Me,
I will heal and give you rest."

A heart poured out to Christ;
Comfort, healing, and rest given;
This heart now sings praises.

A heart shares Christ's love and comfort
To others who are broken and hurting.
Love and compassion is my Master's touch.

Written by Corinne McCoy

The Lord Bless You

The Lord bless you
Who walk in the law of the Lord
And meditate on it day and night.

The Lord bless you
Who commits your life to Him;
He will set His shield around you.

The Lord bless you
Who keep His commandments
And walk in the light of His truth.

The Lord bless you
Who wait patiently for His return
To take His people home.

The Lord Be Praised

From the rising of the sun
To the setting of the same,
The Lord be praised.

Be still, and listen
As the mountains and hills
Praise the Lord on High.

Listen and hear
The rivers, creeks, and oceans
Sing their praises unto the Lord.

Be still, and listen;
The trees, flowers, and all plants
Dance in praise to the Lord.

Listen and hear
As all the animals
Give praise unto the Lord.

Be still and listen
To all of creation
Raising praises unto the Lord.

From the rising of the sun
To the setting of the same
The Lord be praised forever.

Psalm 113:3

From the rising of the sun to its setting,
the name of the Lord is to be praised.

Love

What is Love?
Where can Love be found?
And, why is Love so important?

Love is caring for someone special,
Forgiving people who hurt us,
Accepting someone for who and what they are.

Love is taking time to be a friend,
Taking time to listen,
Taking time to hold someone close.

Love can be found inside yourself,
In the eyes of a child,
And in someone who listens to you.

Love can be found in a flower,
In the trees, in the mountains,
And in the gentleness of animals.

Love is important, because –
Without Love we are empty,
And friends would not be found.

Love is important, because –
The beauty we see, would be no more,
No flowers, no trees, and no mountains.

Most of all, God loves us, and is always with us.
God cares, forgives, and accepts us,
No matter who and what we are.

Jesus

Jesus, born of a virgin,
Ten little toes
Ten little fingers
Born perfect in every way.

Jesus, born as fully man;
Born as fully God.
He grew and learned
As any other baby.

Jesus learned to crawl,
He learned to walk,
He learned to talk and play
As other babies do.

As Jesus grew,
He learned to read and write;
He was obedient to His earthly parents;
He pleased His Heavenly Father.

Jesus grew in wisdom and stature.
His life was our example to live by,
He died as a sacrifice in our place
That we might live for Him.

God Sent His Son

God sent His Son,
A little Baby to be;
Born of a virgin.

God sent His only begotten Son,
Jesus; To grow and learn
As other children learn.

God sent His Son
To teach us of His
Father's love.

God sent His Son
To die on a cross
For you and me.

God sent His Son
To rise up from the grave
So you and I can live with Him forever.

God will send His Son, Jesus
To take His children home
To live forever in heaven with Him.

My Little Child

You are precious, my little child,
You bring joy to my heart,
Your love is full of trust.

You are special, my little child,
Like stars, your eyes sparkle,
Your laughter is like sweet music.

You are unique, my little child,
For no one else has your smile;
No one else has your personality.

You are precious to Jesus, my little child,
You are His gift to me,
To raise you to love Him.

You are special to Jesus, my little child;
For He created you to be unique,
With gifts special to you.

As you grow to know Jesus,
May He bless you in many ways.
With all my love, I give you to Jesus.

John 15:13

Greater love has no man than this,
that a man lay down his life
for his friends.

Greater Love

Greater love has no one
Than to lay down his life
For his friends.

Jesus was beaten beyond recognition,
He was spat upon and mocked.
This He did for you and me.

Jesus showed us how great is
His love for us when
He stretched out His arms on the cross.

As Jesus hung on the cross,
He cried, "Father, forgive them,
For they know not what they do."

How much greater could Jesus' love be;
Than to die such a cruel death;
A death met for you and me.

In A Garden

In a garden far away,
    And many years ago;
A man went to pray
    To His Father in heaven.

He prayed for the Jews
    And Gentiles alike.
He prayed for His disciples,
    For they would continue His work.

This man prayed for the last time;
    In this garden many years ago.
His human part in pain and agony,
    Knowing His time was near.

As He prayed, "Father, if it be possible,
    let this cup pass from me; never the less,
    not my will, but thy will be done."
An angel came to strengthen Him.

As this man prayed more earnestly;
    His sweat became like great drops of blood
    Falling upon the ground.
He rose from prayer and completed His work.

This garden, is Gethsemane –
    A place called Mount of Olives;
This man, is Jesus, God's Son –
    Your Lord and Savior, and mine.

Forgive Them

Hanging on a cross, Jesus prayed,
"Father, forgive them for they
Do not know what they do."

Jesus forgave those who falsely accused Him,
Beat, mocked, and crucified Him.
Peter denied knowing Jesus and was forgiven.

When people hurt you;
When they persecute you;
Will you forgive them?

When you are wronged,
Will you forgive others
As Jesus has forgiven you?
Forgive them.

Jesus' Love

How do you describe Jesus' love?
A love that brought Him to earth
As a Baby in a manger?

How do you describe a love
That shows compassion?
A Love that heals our hearts?

How do you describe a love
That forgives our sins?
A love that heals physical illness?

How do you describe Jesus' love?
A love that He would die for us,
And rise up from the grave?

How do you describe Jesus' love?
A love that pursues and calls to us,
To bring us to Him?

How do you describe unconditional love?
I describe it, our Heavenly Father, Jesus, and Holy Spirit,
No greater love can there be.

Written by Corinne McCoy

Power Of God's Love

What power does love have,
That God would send His only Son,
To live in a world of sin?

The power of Jesus love
Healed the broken hearted, the blind,
The lame, the lepers, the paralyzed, the sick.

This powerful love of Jesus
Raised the dead and cast out demons,
Made the deaf hear and the mute speak.

With the power of love
Jesus fed the multitudes
With a little boy's lunch.

What kind of power does love have,
That held Jesus on a cross to die,
And rise from the grave and live?

The power of the Father's love through Jesus
Has provided the Way to the Father;
Has given the Truth of the Father;
Has given life everlasting with the Father;
This is the Power of God's Love.

Proverbs 3:5-6

Trust in the Lord with all your heart,
and do not rely on your own insight.
 In all your ways acknowledge Him,
and He will make straight your paths.

Trust Me

My heart was in deep despair,
With trouble all around,
I could not see a way out.

I looked for help around me,
And found no one cared,
I felt lost, alone, and afraid.

"Please help me!" I cried.
I heard someone say,
"Trust Me, I will guide you all the way."

I turned and saw no one;
With tears I asked, "Who are You?"
"I am Jesus, My Child."

"Trust Me with all your heart;
I will fill your heart with My peace;
I will never leave nor forsake you."

I trusted and gave my whole heart to Jesus;
My heart He did cleanse,
And filled me with love, joy, and peace;
Jesus is my Guide and Stay forever.

A Life Changed

"Why would You want me, Jesus?
I am wretched and sinful;
I'm selfish and destructive;
I'm full of hate and anger.

"Why do you want me?
I am weak and worthless;
I'm filled with pain and discontent;
I'm lonely and in deep despair."

"Who am I, Jesus, Who am I?
That You would want
This wretched soul of mine?
I am not worthy of You, Jesus."

"Child, I love you," Jesus replied.
"I died in your place,
And rose from the grave
That you may live with Me."

I asked Jesus to forgive me;
He cleansed and filled my heart with love;
He taught me forgiveness, faith and truth;
Jesus changed my life forever.

Tell Me Your Heart

I was walking one day;
My heart heavy with
Pain and loneliness;
No one to listen to me.

Jesus found me,
And walked with me awhile.
"I feel your pain," He said.
"Tell Me your heart."

Where do I start," I replied;
"My pain is so great."
"I will listen My child,
Tell Me Your heart."

I told Jesus of my loss,
And the loneliness I felt.
As I talked, He listened,
And He wiped the tears from my eyes.

Then He said, "Give Me your heart,
And I will make it new."
I gave Jesus my heart,
And He made me whole.

Give Me Your Heart

Jesus saw my heart,
Broken, shattered, and hurting;
In deep despair my heart was;
No one to care was found.

Jesus' heart was full of compassion,
He turned to me and said,
"Give me your heart,
My Child, I care about you."

I replied, "Why You, Lord?
No one else cares, why You?"
I bowed my head and cried,
"Why should You care for me?"

Jesus answered, "I prayed for you,
My Child, I died for you.
Give Me your heart,
My Child, I Love you."

As tears filled my eyes, I whispered,
"My heart is Yours,
I lay my broken heart,
My life at Your feet."

Written by Corinne McCoy

Jesus took my broken heart,
He mended shattered pieces and pain.
Jesus took my despair and
Filled my heart with His love and peace.

Take My Heart, Jesus

Take my heart, Jesus,
Make it Yours;
Heal my broken heart
Till peaceful it becomes.

Heavenly Father, take my heart,
 It is Yours;
Fill my heart with Your Spirit,
Till love overflowing it becomes.

Take my heart, my Lord,
I give it to You;
To serve You my heart is committed
Till You come again.

Take my heart, Jesus,
Make it Yours;
For to You alone it belongs
Take my heart, Lord Jesus.

Come To Me

I heard Jesus say, "Come to Me,
You whose heart is heavy,
And I will give you rest.
My yoke is easy and My burden light."

I bowed my head and said,
"Forgive me, my Lord,
My heart is heavy and filled with sin.
I'm not worthy to be in your presence."

My Savior replied, "My Child,
I have loved you always,
I will forgive your sins,
I will take your burdens away."

"Forgive my sins, my Savior,
Take my burdens far from me,
And fill my heart with your presence,"
Came my heart's cry.

My Lord and my Savior
Forgave me my sins and took my burdens,
He filled my heart with
His peace, His love, and His Spirit.

Matthew 11:28-30

Come to me, all who labor and are heavy laden, and I will
give you rest. Take my yoke upon you, and learn from me;
for I am gentle and lowly in heart, and you will find rest
for your souls. For my yoke is easy, and my burden is light.

Written by Corinne McCoy

Amidst Life's Storms

Amidst life's Storms;
Turn to Jesus,
Trust Him to calm
The winds and waves.

Amidst life's storms;
Put your faith in God –
Faith that He will make sense
Of the chaos in your life.

Amidst the storms of life;
To you who ask for help,
Peace, Jesus does give
Amidst life's storms.

Trust Jesus

Trust Jesus' heart,
He will straighten your path,
And guide you always.

Trust Jesus with your life,
He will give you His peace,
And fill you with His joy.

Trust Jesus with your problems,
 He will protect you,
And guide you through them.

Trust Jesus with all you have;
He will keep you from harm;
Safe in His arms you will be.

Trust Jesus with all your heart,
He will not fail you,
Nor forsake you.

Written by Corinne McCoy

Come To Jesus

Is your heart weary and heavy?
Are you longing for rest and peace?
Is your life troubled
And do not know where to turn?

Come to Jesus, my friend;
He will give you His peace;
He will lighten your burdens;
He will help you through your troubles.

Come to Jesus
And ask Him to come into your heart;
Pour out your heart to Him;
He will take your cares and burdens away.

O weary one, Jesus loves you.
On bended knee, come to Jesus.
Talk with Him, He will listen;
He will heal and forgive you.

Be Still

Why are you restless?
O my soul,
Where is your faith?

Be still, my soul and listen;
Listen with all your heart and mind;
Give ear to the Lord your God.

Be still, my soul,
In reverence and awe,
For the Lord your God is near.

Be still, my soul,
Have complete faith in Jesus,
Trust Him completely.

O my soul, be still,
For Jesus loves you,
He will guide and protect you.

Be still, my soul, and listen,
For you belong to Jesus,
Be still, my soul, be still.

Thank You, Father

Heavenly Father, You've reached
Into the depths of my despair,
And brought me back to you.

You have taken my broken heart;
Put the pieces together,
And healed my heart.

You have searched my soul;
Found deep darkness inside,
You cleansed and made me whole.

Father, thank You,
For healing my heart,
And cleansing my soul.

Thank You, Father,
For caring enough to save me;
For loving me as I am.

Psalm 34:18

The Lord is near
to the broken hearted,
and saves the crushed in Spirit.

Peace, Be Still

Is your heart raging with storms –
Storms of worry, storms of anger?
Tell Jesus about it.
"Peace, be still", He will say.

Is your mind filled with storms –
Storms of hatred, storms of fear?
Tell Jesus about it.
He will say, "Peace, be still."

Peace, Jesus will give your heart;
Peace, He will give your mind;
Peace in your life Jesus will give.
Peace, be still.

Peace, be still –
"Be still and know I am God.
My peace I will give you."
Peace, Be Still.

Jesus Is Waiting

Jesus is pleading with you –
Pleading for you to Him come;
He wants your heart to cleanse –
To wash it white as snow.

Come to Jesus, He wants you;
Ask Him to forgive your sins;
Ask Him to live in your heart;
His peace He will give you.

He wants to teach you
Of His love for you;
Of His mercy for you;
Of the Heavenly Father's love.

Will you ask Jesus to come in?
Are you willing to give Him
All your heart, mind, soul, and strength?
Jesus is waiting and longing for you.

Written by Corinne McCoy

I'm Yours

Holy Father in heaven,
Take my heart,
Make it Yours,
To love and care for others.

Take my hands,
Use them to serve You,
To help others,
To glorify You in all I do.

Take my feet,
Guide them down
The path You have
Chosen for me.

Take my mouth,
Put Your words in it
To bring honor and
Glory and praise to you.

Take my mind,
Put Your thoughts in it,
Teach me Your will
That I may live for You.
Holy Father, I'm Yours.

Teach My Heart

Heavenly Father, my Lord and Savior,

Teach my heart Your righteousness,
That I may live it.

Teach my heart to love
As You love.

Teach my heart compassion
As You showed compassion.

Teach my heart to forgive
As You forgive.

Teach my heart to see
With Your eyes.

Teach my heart Your ways,
That I may live according to Your Word.

Teach my heart Your will for my life,
So I may live in it.

For You are my God, my King,
And my Life forever. Amen.

A Prayer

Heavenly Father,
Forgive me, I pray –
Forgive my sins.
Take my heart and make it Yours.

Cleanse my heart, O Lord,
Remove any wicked way in me;
Fill me with Your Holy Spirit,
And grant me Your peace.

Show me Your ways,
O Lord, That I may follow You,
And guide me into all truth,
That I may live it.

Freely, I give my whole heart;
For with You I desire
To walk in Your light
And Your love and care.

Not my will, Father, but Your will
Be done in my life.
This I ask in Jesus Holy name,
Amen.

Here Is My Heart

Here is my heart, Jesus,
Cleanse it from sin,
That You may live in it.

Here is my mind, Father,
Put Your thoughts in it,
That I may do Your will.

Here are my hands, Lord,
I give them to You,
To serve others for You.

Here are my feet, Father,
Guide them in the path
You choose for me.

Here is my life, Father,
Use it to praise You –
To bring honor and glory to You.

To You alone, Jesus,
I desire to surrender –
To surrender my all to You.

James 4:7

Submit yourselves therefore to God.
Resist the devil and he will flee from you.

God's Heart

God loves each one of us, you know;
He desires a heart submissive
And obedient to His will.

God's heart is compassionate enough
To heal our hurts and pains,
To comfort when needed.

God's heart is wise enough
To take care of us,
To guide each one down our path.

God's heart loves enough
To take us in His arms,
To strengthen and encourage us.

God's heart rejoices
When we have faith, believe, and trust;
When we obey and submit to His will.

Faith Is

Faith is believing without seeing.
Believe Jesus is always with you;
Believe He will guide you.

Faith is trusting God.
Trust Him to help you
Through both tough and good times.

Faith is obeying God.
Obey God in all you do;
You will see wondrous things.

Faith is the substance
Of things hoped for.
Give your dreams and desires to God.

Faith is following Jesus.
Jesus will lead you in paths of
Righteousness and peace.

Give Praise

O my soul, give praise.
Give praise to Jesus,
For He has saved you;
He has given you life everlasting.

Give praise to the Father,
For He has healed your heart.
He has mended and made you whole.
He has brought you into His family.

Give praise to the Holy Spirit,
For He teaches you of the Father;
And leads you into all understanding;
He guides you to obey the Father.

Give praise, O my soul;
By the blood of the Lamb,
You have been redeemed.
Through faith in Jesus you are saved.

The Father loves you;
Jesus has taken your sins away;
The Holy Spirit lives in you;
Give praise, my soul, give praise.

Commit Your Life

Commit your way to the Lord;
<u>He will guide your path.</u>
Trust Him.

Commit your heart to Jesus;
Listen to His quiet voice.
Obey Him.

Commit your soul to God;
He will help you through tough times.
Trust Him.

Commit all you do to the Lord;
He will direct your decisions.
Have faith in Him.

Commit your life to Jesus;
He will bless you.
Draw close to God.

Psalm 37:5

Commit your way to the Lord;
trust in Him and He will act.

Proverbs 16:3

Commit your work to the Lord,
and your plans will be established.

1 Peter 4:19

Therefore, let those who suffer
according to God's will do right
and entrust their souls to a faithful Creator.

Written by Corinne McCoy

He Will Not Fail You

Trust in God's infinite wisdom;
He alone knows what is in your heart;
He alone knows what is ahead.
Trust Him, He will not fail you.

Turn to the Father,
At His feet, leave all your cares;
He will supply all your needs
He will not fail you.

In heaven, store your treasures;
For there, your heart will be;
God will guide and protect you;
He will not fail you.

Do Not Pass Me

Do not pass me, Jesus;
Forgive me my sins,
Save me, Jesus, save me.

Come into my broken heart,
Come in to stay,
Come in to live forever.

Do not pass me, Jesus,
When on others you call,
Do not pass me.

Do not pass me,
Gentle Lord, gentle Savior, gentle Father;
Do not pass by me.

Surrender To God

Surrender to God,
Accept Jesus as your Savior;
Let Him guide you
To complete surrender.

Through Jesus, build your
Relationship with God;
Peace and eternal life
Our Heavenly Father will give.

Step out in faith;
Jesus is waiting for you;
He will never leave you
Nor forsake you.

Surrender your all to God;
You will not be disappointed;
O sinner, God loves you;
Will you completely surrender to Him?

Love God

Love God with all your heart;
Love Him with all your soul;
Love Him with all your mind.

To love God is to obey Him;
To love Him is to trust Him;
To love Him is to have faith in Him.

Love God and keep all His commandments;
Love Him and worship Him in song;
Love Him and bow in reverence.

Love God and give glory to Him;
Love Him and give Him Praise;
Love Him and give Him honor.

Show God's love by serving others;
Show His love by forgiving others;
Show His love by encouraging others.

Written by Corinne McCoy

I Will Praise You

Father, I praise You in the morning,
For You have brought
Joy into my life.

I will sing praises to You,
For You have filled
My heart with music.

I will praise You at noon,
For You have filled
Me with Your love.

I will give You praise
For You have filled
Me with Your peace.

I will praise You in the evening,
For You have given
Me life everlasting.

You are my Fortress and my Refuge;
With my whole heart,
I will praise You.

Rejoice In Our Lord

The rivers and streams sing songs of joy,
As they rush to meet the lakes and oceans;
The trees and flowers raise all their beauty and splendor,
As they reach up to heaven.

The birds sing their songs of praise;
The creatures in the waters and animals of the land
Raise their hearts in love;
Listen as each rejoices in the Lord in their own way.

We have much to be thankful for;
God has given us the beauty we see
In the mountains, trees, flowers,
And all the animals, lakes and rivers.

God has made us in His image;
Through Jesus, His Son, He has shown us
How much we are to love each other.

God has truly blessed us, because --
We will live with Him in Glory forever;
With all of creation, let us sing praises.
Rejoice in our Lord forever.

Written by Corinne McCoy

My Father's Mountains

I climbed a hill tonight –
To enjoy the snow covered
Mountains around me.

The moon shines in all its splendor;
And the stars shine like candles
As they light up the mountains.

I see the beauty in the mountains
As they stand in all their majesty –
Earth's alters unto God.

In the stillness of the night,
I can hear God's voice
Speaking soft and gentle.

It is here, on this hill,
When I feel closest to God
For there are no walls between us.

It is here, on this hill,
I speak from my heart with God, my Father,
And I listen to Him.

It is here, on this hill,
I stand in awe, as I see and feel
The beauty in my Father's mountains.

Jesus, My Lord

Jesus, Lord of all.
He came from heaven
My soul to find –
And found a heart filled with pain.

Jesus said, "Come and rest."
He took away the pain
And gave peace in its place.
Now Jesus is Lord of my life forever.

My Heavenly Father's Touch

My Heavenly Father touched the sky;
Rain fell and watered the earth,
Rivers and lakes it did create.

My Father touched the flowers;
In many colors their beauty did give,
Bringing glory unto God.

My Father touched the trees;
Reaching high into the sky,
Pointing toward heaven.

My Father touched the mountains;
In Beauty they became
Majestic alters unto Him.

My Father walks with the wild;
Shelter and food He gives the animals,
They give Him honor, glory, and praise.

My Father saw my broken heart;
He healed and filled my heart with joy and love;
This is my Heavenly Father's touch.

My Lord, My God

O Lord, You are my God.
I praise You for Your saving grace;
You have given me new life.

O God, You are my Lord.
I will praise You for the joy
You have bestowed on me.

My Lord, my God,
You sent Your Son
To show me the way to You.

O Lord, You are my God.
Thank You for taking
My sins to the cross.

God, You are my Lord.
In my heart Your peace did give.
For this, I will glorify You.

My Lord, my God.
I give You honor, praise, and glory
All the days of my life.

Will You Love God?

Will you serve God
At home and work
With your gifts and talents?

Will you glorify God
In all you do,
No matter what happens?
Will you love God?

Will you give praise to God
In the good times
And in the bad times?
Will you love God?

Will you love God
With all your heart and mind?
With all your strength?
Will you love God?

One Heart At A Time

One heart changed for Jesus;
With praise and thanksgiving
Heavenly angels rejoice.

Another heart softens to His voice;
Listen and hear Jesus calling –
Calling, "Come home to Me."

A heart touched by Jesus,
Guided by His Spirit,
Follows where He leads.

One heart broken;
Jesus mends the pieces;
The heart is healed.

Another heart is hurting,
Comfort and peace,
Jesus does give.

With love, patience, and gentleness,
Jesus brings to the Father,
One heart at a time.

Search My Heart

O Lord, my God, search my heart,
If there be any wicked way in me,
Remove it and fill me with Your Holy Spirit.

Cleanse my heart of any sinful way,
Restore me to the joy of Your salvation,
O Lord, restore my heart to Your ways.

Search me, O God and know my heart;
Try me and know my thoughts;
Bring me into Your tender mercies.

Place in my heart Your love,
That I may love as You love,
And see others with Your eyes.

Write on my heart Your word;
Place in my mind Your thoughts;
And a desire to know You more.

Search my heart, Lord Jesus,
Give me a desire to know Your will,
And a desire to obey You.

O Lord, I Pray

Fill me with Your Spirit, O God,
That I may bring glory, praise,
And honor to You, my King.

I sing praises to You, my God,
For You have filled my soul with
Overflowing joy of thanksgiving.

You, O Lord, have given me
A peace within my heart;
A peace that will last forever and ever.

Fill me with Your Spirit,
That I may bring honor, praise, and
Glory to You, my Heavenly Father.

Grant that I may know
Your will for my life;
Show me Your path for me.

In all Your ways, O Lord,
Direct my path to follow You;
O Lord, my Father, I pray.

Peace

My soul is restless,
Like a storm raging inside;
Or a rushing river.
My soul, Jesus quiets.

Peace, Jesus gives;
A peace the world cannot give;
Peace the world does not understand;
A peace the world does not know.

Peaceful my soul becomes,
When Jesus fills my heart with love;
Forgiving is my Savior,
As joy fills my life.

When Jesus is near,
Life's storms become peaceful,
And the river of life becomes calm.
Jesus gives me His peace.

Take My Hand

Take my heart, Heavenly Father, purify me,
Purify my soul to live with You,
Prepare me to live forever in heaven.

Take my hand, Holy Spirit, guide me,
Guide me into the Father's light,
Guide me through the hard times.

Take my hand, Jesus, lead me,
Lead me into Your will,
Lead me through the dark times.

Take my heart, Heavenly Father, purify me.
Take my hand, Holy Spirit, guide me.
Take my hand, Jesus, lead me.

Galatians 5:22-23

But the fruit of the Spirit is
love, joy, peace, patience,
kindness, goodness, faithfulness,
gentleness, self-control;
against such there is no law.

Fruit Of The Spirit

Love the Lord your God
With all your heart, soul, and mind;
Love your neighbor as yourself;
God's peace and joy will be yours.

Be patient in all you do;
Show kindness to those who hurt you;
And do good to your enemies.

Be gentle to those who are hurting;
Control yourself in what you think, say, and do;
Stay faithful to God in everything;
He will bless you with many blessings.

Teach Me

Lord, teach me to forgive –
To forgive others
As You have forgiven me.

Father, teach me to see –
To see people
Through Your eyes.

Jesus, teach me to serve –
To serve those in need
As You willingly served.

Lord, teach me Your word –
To live as You have shown me;
To live as Your word teaches me.

Father, teach me to love –
To love as You love;
To love with all my heart, soul, and mind.

Walk With Jesus

Take time to walk with Jesus;
Through His word, listen to Him;
Let Jesus guide your life.

Take time to walk with Jesus;
Tell Him your heart's concerns;
He will answer your prayers.

Take time to walk with Jesus;
Walk quietly beside Him,
Listen as He speaks softly to you.

Take time to walk with Jesus;
Give Him your heart's pain,
He will heal and give you peace.

Take time to walk with Jesus;
Draw near to Him,
His overflowing joy will be in you.

Written by Corinne McCoy

The Lord Is My Everything

There is joy in my soul;
For the Lord is my song;
He is my hope and my salvation;
He is my Savior in whom I surrender.

There is love in my life;
For the Lord is my heart's desire;
He is my strength in my weakness;
He is my Heavenly Father whom I will obey.

There is faith in my heart;
For the Lord is my shield;
He is my rock and my fortress;
He is my King in whom I trust.

There is joy in my soul;
There is love in my life;
There is faith in my heart;
For the Lord is my Everything.

Thankfulness

Unto your Heavenly Father,
Bend your knee in thankfulness;
For He has given you life.

In thankfulness, praise the Father;
He answers every prayer
You have prayed to Him.

In thankfulness, sing to the Lord,
Bringing glory and honor unto Him;
He will fill you with everlasting joy.

In thankfulness, serve God;
Give to Him your best;
Give Him all your heart.

In thankfulness, love Jesus;
Keep all of His commandments;
Love Him with all your heart and soul.

In thankfulness, trust God;
He will fill your life with
Blessings of love and happiness.

Written by Corinne McCoy

Bless The Lord

Bless the Lord, my soul;
He is my rock and my salvation;
In Him will I put my trust.

I will bless the Lord,
His mercies are true and just,
His loving kindness is pure.

Blessed be the Lord,
He has heard my cry
And answered my prayer.

Bless the Lord, my soul;
He is my strength and my shield,
Of whom shall I be afraid?

Remember

Though times are hard,
And all seems lost;
Though the enemy surrounds you;
Remember, God is near and will take care of you.

Though Satan accuses you,
And in prison you are tossed;
Though the end seems far away,
Remember, trust God to take you through.

Though many dangers are all around;
Though there is pestilence and famine,
Though there is strife in the land,
Remember, trust God to protect you always.

Remember, keep strong your faith in God,
He will never fail you.
Remember, keep strong your trust in God,
His love for you will never fail.

Written by Corinne McCoy

God's Spirit

God's Spirit fills the forest with music.
Be still, and listen –
Listen to the praises the forest sings –
Praises of love, honor, joy, and peace.

As God fills the forest with His Spirit;
So shall He fill our hearts;
With music and praises of honor and love.
We need only ask His Spirit to fill us.

Come, Holy Spirit, Come

Come, Holy Spirit, come
Cleanse and purify my heart,
Come in my heart to dwell.

Come, Holy Spirit, come
Teach me of Jesus,
Teach me of the Father.

Come, Holy Spirit, come
Lead me into Truth,
Lead me into understanding.

Come, Holy Spirit, come
Guide my footsteps down the path
That pleases the Father.

Come, Holy Spirit, come
Fill my heart with the Father's love,
That I may follow my Father's will.

Written by Corinne McCoy

Keep Focused On Jesus

Look to Jesus for salvation;
He and He alone will save you
He will forgive and cleanse you from sin.

Keep your eyes on Jesus;
Soften your heart toward Him,
For to your heart He will speak.

Keep focused on Jesus;
Through storms of life He will guide
In times of trials, He will help.

Stay focused on Jesus;
When you stumble and fall,
He will lift you up and help you stand.

Keep your eyes on Jesus;
He will give you rest
When you are tired and weary.

Keep focused on Jesus;
Cast all your cares on Him,
He will give you peace.

People Of God

Where is your heart, people of God?
Write His word upon your hearts;
Grow in your love for Him;
Love Him and Keep all His commandments.

Where is your faith in God?
Is it rooted deep in His word?
Strengthen your faith in Him,
And you will grow closer to Him.

People of God,
Do you trust Him enough
To let Him guide you
Through earth's final days?

Dear people of God,
Are you ready for Jesus' return?
Prepare your hearts, minds, and souls;
He is coming soon to take us home.

Why Do You Wait?

You who are wicked,
Come to Jesus and repent;
While there is still time,
Turn from your evil ways.

Jesus comes soon,
To claim those who are His own,
And take them home;
Home to live forever with Him.

You who are wicked,
Why do you wait to repent?
Tomorrow may be too late;
Put your faith and trust in Jesus.

Jesus cares for you,
He loves you,
He wants to live in your hearts today.
O sinner why do you wait?

Come In, Lord Jesus

"I stand at the door and knock;
Will you let Me in, My Child?
I desire to live in your heart,
Will you let Me in?"

"Your heart I will cleanse.
Ask and your sins I will forgive
And remember no more.
Will you let Me in?"

"Come, Lord Jesus
And wash me white as snow.
Come in, search my heart,
Remove my sins – forgive me."

"Come in, Lord Jesus,
Live in my heart
Fill me and know my thoughts,
Teach me Your ways"

Total Surrender

Take my heart, my mind,
my soul, O Lord, my God,
I surrender all of me to You.

Take my heart and make it Yours,
Take my mind and put Your thoughts in it,
Take my soul to do Your will.

Teach my heart to love as You love,
Teach my mind to say Your words,
Teach my soul to follow You.

Teach my heart to forgive as You forgive,
Teach my mind to encourage others,
Teach my soul to walk where You lead.

Take all I own and make them Yours,
I leave them in Your keeping,
I surrender my all to You alone.

Worship God

Worship God in reverence;
Come to Him on bended knee,
In awe of His Majestic Name.

Worship God in truth;
Trusting His heart to guide;
Having faith in His power to save.

Worship God with praise;
Praise Him with your voice;
Praise Him with all your heart.

Worship God with music;
Singing praises, bringing glory to Him;
Playing instruments to honor Him.

Worship God in all you do;
Serve others as serving God;
Work as you would work for God.

Worship God in spirit;
Come in humbleness,
And sit at His feet in worship.

Blessed Are You

Blessed are you who keep all
The commandments of God;
Take delight in His law,
It is the beginning of wisdom.

Blessed are you whose
Trust is in the Lord;
He is our Guide and Stay;
He is our Refuge and Fortress.

Blessed are you whose
Hope is in Jesus;
His promised return;
We wait with perseverance.

Blessed are you whose
Faith is in Jesus;
Walk in the truth and light
Of God our Father.

Two Trails

Two trails meet;
A friendship begins;
It grows and blossoms.

Love for each other begins;
Love cares, love is patient;
Love is kind and understanding.

Love is giving and cherishing;
Love encourages and strengthens;
Love listens and respects.

Love is faithful and supports;
Love is not jealous or empty;
Love is forgiving.

Love rejoices in truth;
Love believes all things;
Love hopes all things.

Love is from God;
Love never fails;
Two trails become one.

Love Is

Love is from God;
Keep Him in the center of your marriage,
For your love will grow deeper each day.

Love is patient and kind,
Love listens and understands,
Love supports and strengthens.

Love chastises and encourages,
It is not jealous or empty,
Love is forgiving.

Love hopes and cares,
Love respects and gives,
Love never ends.

Love is always faithful;
Love is the very essence –
The very character of God.

Till We Meet Again

My time has come to sleep;
Take time to grieve;
For in death do I sleep,
Till Jesus comes again.

This is not "Good bye,"
But till we meet again,
When we see Jesus;
For now I rest and sleep awhile.

Rejoice and be happy;
Soon Jesus will come
To take us home to live
In heaven with Him forever.

I love you my Daughter;
I love you my Son;
To Jesus draw yourselves close;
To Him follow, listen and obey always;
Till we meet again my children.

Written by Corinne McCoy

A Stranger Am I

A stranger am I,
Journeying through this world –
This world of sin and danger.

A stranger am I,
Longing for heaven and home,
Where peace and harmony is forever.

A stranger am I,
Following where Jesus leads;
Following His path to heaven.

A stranger am I,
Waiting and watching for Jesus' return;
His soon return to take me home.

Power And Majesty

We wait for You, Jesus,
To come and take us home;
We watch and pray.

In Power and Majesty;
As You have promised,
You will come in the clouds.

In Power and Majesty,
Jesus, Satan's defeat will be final;
His evil forces will be gone forever.

In the gentleness of Your Power,
You will reign as King forever;
Jesus, how Majestic Your name.

At home in heaven with You;
In the Power and Majesty of Your love;
Forever in peace to live.

Written by Corinne McCoy

When Will You Come?

Oh Lord, my God, my King,
When will You come for us?
How much longer must we wait?

Jesus, I long to live with You –
With You forever in heaven.
When will You come?

To live in the beautiful city
With streets made of gold.
When will You come?

I long for heaven and home;
I wait and watch for You.
When will You come?

With Jesus, my King, forever;
I long in heaven to be.
When will You come?

Prepare Me

My Heavenly Father, my God,
You are my King forever, my Savior,
You are my Creator, my life;
Prepare me to live in heaven.

Prepare my heart, Lord,
Purify my heart as gold;
Wash me white as snow;
And direct my path to You.

Prepare me for Your Kingdom;
To live in Your beautiful city;
To walk on streets of gold;
To live in the new earth.

Jesus, I want to be ready
When You come, prepare me.
In Your will, keep me;
For Your will I desire to do.

Armor Of God

We do not wrestle against people,
But against Satan and his demons.
Jesus will stand with us against evil.

Belt of Truth, Jesus is Truth;
Speaking and living in Truth
With our lives, God will be pleased.

Breastplate of Righteousness;
Good qualities God gives us;
Jesus will teach us.

Shod your feet with the Gospel of Peace;
God will give us His peace as
We spread His Word to every one.

God's Shield of Faith;
From Satan's firey assaults,
God will protect us.

Helmet of Salvation;
For Jesus' promised return we wait;
God's Sword of the Spirit, His Word;
Teaches us of God and to pray;
Praying always in the Spirit.

Ephesians 6:10-18

Finally, be strong in the Lord and in the strength of His might. Put on the whole armor of God, that you may be able to stand against the wiles of the devil. For we are not contending against flesh and blood, but against the principalities, against the powers, against the world rulers of this present darkness, against the spiritual hosts of wickedness in the heavenly places. Therefore, take the whole armor of God, that you may be able to withstand in the evil day. And having done all to stand. Stand therefore, having girded your loins with truth, and having put on the breastplate of righteousness, and having shod your feet with the equipment of the gospel of peace; above all taking the shield of faith, with which you can quench all the flaming darts of the evil one. And take the helmet of salvation, and the sword of the spirit, which is the word of God. Pray at all times in the Spirit, with all prayer and supplication. To that end keep alert with all perseverance, making supplication for all the saints.

Are You Ready?

Are you ready for Jesus to come?
Is Your heart in tune with God?
Do you listen with the ears of your heart?

Jesus gave us signs of His second coming;
There shall be wars and rumors of wars,
Nations will rise against nations.

Deceptions from Satan will be;
False prophets and teachers shall there be;
There will be tribulations.

Where is your heart?
Do you know God's word?
Do you trust God to give you discernment?

Will you hold fast to God's promises?
Will you endure to the end?
Are you ready for Jesus to come again?

Turn Your Hearts

Beast of power –
Powerful nation, you seek to turn
People to worship the antichrist.

Antichrist who goes against God;
You seek to deceive God's people;
You attempt to change God's law.

You, Dragon, who is Satan,
Deceiver who is an imposter –
Your time will end.

People of God, turn your hearts –
Turn away from the antichrist,
And turn your hearts toward God.

Your full trust in God, keep;
Your lives, completely surrender to God;
He alone can save and protect you.

Who Will You Choose?

The Day of Atonement
Is soon drawing to an end;
The righteous will be sealed by God;
The wicked will bear the beast's mark.

From the wicked
The Holy Spirit will be lifted;
Mercy no longer will be offered;
For the destiny of all will be decided forever.

For God's Word,
A rebellious people will search;
In vain, they will never be filled;
Their cases have been decided.

Probation will soon be closed;
No longer are prayers for the wicked offered;
No mercy for the wicked;
Their fate is decided and unchanged.

Will you be on God's side?
Will you be against God
And suffer the consequences?
Who will you choose to obey?

God Or Man

When the final tribulation comes,
Who will you obey?
God or man?

To change God's laws,
Man has sought;
His Sabbath, he does not keep.

Trouble for God's people;
Tribulation as never known before.
Will your faith in God hold strong?

Through this trouble,
Will you trust God completely?
Will you obey God rather than man?

Revelation 1:7-8

Behold, He is coming with the clouds, and every eye will see Him, everyone who pierced Him; and all tribes of the earth will wail on account of Him. Even so. Amen. "I am the Alpha and the Omega," says the Lord God, who is and who was and who is to come, the Almighty.

Jesus Comes

Look to the east;
For Jesus comes in the clouds;
He comes to take His people home;
Home to live with Him forever.

When Jesus comes for His own
Everyone shall see Him;
He comes in power and Majesty;
His glory shines far and near.

Jesus is the Alpha and Omega;
He is the beginning and the end;
He was at the beginning of creation;
He will be at the end of this earth.

Jesus was before time,
He is with us now,
He will be forever without end.
Jesus comes for His redeemed.

Take Heed

With pains and groans,
Earth's last days is soon to come
As Jesus' return grows near.

The closer to Jesus' return,
Storms become more frequent
And more devastating.

As time grows shorter;
Earthquakes are more often
And more violent.

Take heed to the signs -
Signs of Jesus' soon return –
His return for His people.

Time is quickly growing short
Listen to the earth's groans
Take heed to the signs of the end.

Obedience To God

Man seeks to change God's law;
His commandments,
Null and void to make.

Satan seeks to deceive God's people;
To confuse and destroy His remnant people;
To cause His people to disobey.

Remember God's commandments;
You who love God,
Obey His law completely.

Keep God's laws in your hearts;
Stay strong with all your strength,
With all your mind and soul in God.

For at the end of this age,
It will be most important,
For complete obedience to God.

God Provides

Satan is deceiving many people;
By his accusations
He is persecuting God's people;
God provides protection for His own.

When no food can be found;
No place for shelter is found;
All seems lost and hopeless;
God will provide all our needs.

When earthquakes increase;
When storms and floods increase;
When all kinds of disasters increase;
God will provide a safe place.

When earth's end is here,
And the last plagues come;
Everything seems chaotic;
God will provide a hiding place.

God Or Satan

A day will come when
Two classes of people there be;
Those who have the seal of God;
Those who bear the mark of the beast.

The sealed in God,
Obeys all His commandments;
They worship Him in truth
On His seventh day Sabbath.

They who have the beast's mark,
A false Sabbath
They do worship on;
By Satan, they have been deceived.

Does Satan deceive you?
Do you obey all God's commandments?
Who will you follow?
Will you choose God or Satan?

Send The Rain

Prepare the field,
God will send the rain;
Fields are plowed, seeds are planted,
Rain nourishes the seeds.

Speak of Jesus and His love;
His love for the poor and rich alike;
His compassion for the sick and oppressed;
God will send the rain.

Proclaim the good news;
Of Jesus life, death, and resurrection;
Of the peace that only He can give;
God will send the rain.

Tell of Jesus' promised return;
Of the new heaven and new earth;
Where sin, pain, and parting will never be.
The rain will come.

Prepare the field –
God will send the rain.

Seal Of God

God will put His seal upon
Those who keep the true Sabbath;
The fourth commandment Sabbath.

When probation ends;
All God's people will be sealed.
Will you be one of them?

Soon it will be too late
To choose to follow God;
To follow Him is to surrender all to Him.

Children of God,
If you truly love Him,
All His commandments obey.

You who keep God's true Sabbath;
It is His covenant between you and Him;
For the true Sabbath is the Seal of God.

Babylon

Babylon, wicked city of old;
With idolatry and
All kinds of evil is filled.

Old Babylon is now gone,
A spiritual Babylon has risen;
A wicked and deceitful Babylon.

You hide yourself well, Babylon;
Pretending from God to be,
Of your sins, you make the people drink.

From Babylon, the wicked church,
God calls to His people,
"Come, My people, come out of her."

God's people hear His voice,
From wicked places they come;
The cry, "Babylon is fallen" is heard.

Revelation 18:2-4

And he called out with mighty voice, "Fallen, fallen is Babylon the great! It has become a dwelling place of demons, a haunt of every foul spirit, a haunt of every foul and hateful bird; for all nations have drunk the wine of her impure passion, and the kings of the earth have committed fornication with her, and the merchants of the earth have grown rich with the wealth of her wantonness." Then I heard another voice from heaven saying, "Come out of her, My people, lest you take part in their sins, lest you share in her plagues.

Seven Last Plagues

The day of judgment ends;
On those who worship the beast;
Earth's final plagues begin.

Terrible, painful sores appear;
Sea creatures die as the sea turns to blood;
To blood, rivers and springs turn.

To scorch people, the sun is given power;
As God's light protects His people,
Deep darkness falls upon the earth.

Evil spirits deceive rulers of the earth,
They join Satan against heaven;
Soon, the final conflict of good and evil will end.

Around the world, an earthquake shakes;
Mountains and islands disappear;
Great hail destroys all that lives.

Seven last plagues have ended;
Christ comes for His people
Who have been protected.

Take Us Home

Through the clouds,
There's a gate into
A new earth where
Jesus will take us home.

Home where the trees
Grow straight and tall;
And the flowers of many colors
Will never fade or die.

In the meadows where
The soft green grass
Grows rich and sweet
Beneath your feet.

The mountains hold
A beauty all their own
As they stand
In grace and majesty.

Home where everyone and everything
Lives in peace and harmony.
Come and take us home, Jesus,
Take us home where we belong.

Home With Jesus

A wonderful day it will be
When Jesus we see;
To live with Him
In our heavenly home
Forever to be.

A hug I long to give Jesus;
To thank Him face to face,
For loving me;
For saving my life;
For bringing me home to Him.

The only signs of the earth gone by;
Are the scars Jesus bears;
Scars of thorns upon His head;
A scar from the spear in His side;
Scars in His hands and feet from the nails.

How I long to hug and thank Jesus;
For cleansing my heart;
For teaching me to forgive and love;
For showing me the way home;
Alas, at home with Jesus.

With Majesty And Love

In power and majesty,
Jesus will return
To claim His own,
With Him to live forever.

With power, Jesus will defeat Satan.
In the new heaven
And the new earth,
Sin will be no more.

With majesty and love,
Jesus will reign forever
In the new heaven and new earth,
Death, pain, and tears will never be.

In power and majesty,
God's light will shine forever;
In the new heaven and new earth,
Love, peace, and joy will be forever.

1 Thessalonians 4:16-17

For the Lord Himself will descend from heaven with a cry of command, with the archangel's call, and with the sound of the trumpet of God. And the dead in Christ will rise first; then we who are alive; who are left, shall be caught up together with them in the clouds to meet the Lord in the air; and so we shall always be with the Lord.

Christ Comes

From the eastern sky,
With a shout and trumpet blast,
With tens of thousands of angels,
Christ will come in the clouds.

Christ comes in Power and Majesty;
He comes as the Lion of Judah
And the Lamb that was slain;
Slain for all who believe in Him.

With the voice of an archangel,
Christ comes in glory and victory;
Coming for those sleeping in His name,
He comes for all who are sealed in God.

From prison cells and bondage,
From the deepest sea,
And from earth's hidden places,
Christ comes to take His people home.

Desolation

The earth is desolate,
Everything in ruins – shambles.

Cities and towns in rubble are;
Foundations of the earth by earthquake shaken.

Millions of uprooted trees
On the ground lay - destroyed.

From the depths of the seas and earth,
Rocks are scattered upon dry land.

Huge holes left where
Mountains once stood majestically.

The earth is a wilderness;
A desert, lonely, dry, and dusty;
Uninhabited – desolation.

Revelation 16:17 – 21

Then the seventh angel poured out his bowl into the air, and a loud voice came out of the temple of heaven, from the throne, saying, "It is done!" And there were noises and thunderings and lightenings; and there was a great earthquake, such a mighty and great earthquake as had not occurred since men were on the earth. Now the great city was divided into three parts, and the cities of the nation's fell. And great Babylon was remembered before God, to give her the cup of the wine of the fierceness of His wrath. Then every island fled away, and the mountains were not found. And great hail from heaven fell upon men, each hailstone about the weight of a talent. Men blasphemed God because of the plague of the hail, since that plague was exceedingly great.

Revelation 20:1-6

Then I saw an angel coming down from heaven, holding in his hand the key of the bottomless pit and a great chain. And he seized the dragon, that ancient serpent, who is the devil and Satan, and bound him for a thousand years, and threw him into the pit, and shut it and sealed it over him, that he should deceive the nations no more, till the thousand years were ended. After that he must be loosed for a little while. Then I saw thrones, and seated on them were those to whom judgment was committed. Also, I saw the souls of those who had been beheaded for their testimony to Jesus and for the word of God, and who had not worshiped the beast or its image and had not received its mark on their foreheads or their hands. They came to life and reigned with Christ a thousand years. The rest of the dead did not come to life until the thousand years were ended. This is the first resurrection. Blessed and holy is he who shares in the first resurrection! Over such the second death has no power, but they shall be priests of God and of Christ, and they shall reign with Him a thousand years.

1,000 Years

The dead in Christ arise;
With the living saints,
All are changed in a moment.

Infants to their mothers are returned;
Friends and families are reunited,
Never to part again.

With songs of rejoicing,
Christ takes all who are His
To the City of God – the New Jerusalem.

In heaven with Christ,
The righteous shall reign
To judge the wicked 1,000 years.

The wicked destroyed, the earth lay desolate;
To the earth, Satan is bound 1,000 years
To see the result of his rebellion.

A Song Is Given

To each of us a song is given;
A song is given to birds of the air;
To all land animals a song is given;
A song is given to all sea creatures.

A song of praise to God our Creator;
A song to honor God our Father;
A song glorifying God our Savior;
A song of faith in God our Protector.

Sing joyfully to the Lord;
Let our songs rise above the clouds
And bless the Lord, our Father,
As they touch His heart.

Oh wonderful day,
When in heaven we sing
With the angels a new song –
A new song given to each of us.

Holy City Of God

Jerusalem, beautiful city of God
Coming down from heaven;
Sin no longer enters your gates;
For sin will be no more.

Many rooms Jesus has prepared;
Rooms for His people to live;
To live in peace forever;
How wonderful it will be.

Oh, holy city that shines bright;
Colors of the rainbow surrounds you;
How joyous to live with God;
To worship and praise Him forever.

Oh holy city of God,
How beautiful you are;
Your light reflects His glory –
Glory that shines only from God.

The New Earth

The old earth is no more. From all wickedness,
The earth is purified
By an all consuming fire.

A new heaven and earth
Replaces the old heaven and earth.
Everything is fresh and new;
No sin, no dying, no sadness.

Rivers and lakes are crystal clear;
Mountains once again stand majestically;
Trees and all plants are straight and beautiful;
All animals are gentle and friendly.

A new earth God has created;
A place where love, joy, and peace abound;
A place where God's people abide together.
This is the new earth.

Revelation 21:1

Then I saw a new heaven and a new earth;
for the first heaven and the first earth had passed away;
and the sea was no more.

Written by Corinne McCoy

Eden Is Restored

One thousand years has ended;
The wicked raised from death;
Satan, his demons, and the wicked,
By an all consuming fire are destroyed.

The New Jerusalem descends from heaven;
From all evil, the earth is cleansed,
And is created new;
No more pain, no sorrow, no death.

From God's throne, a river flows,
Giving life to the new earth.
On both sides, the tree of life grows,
Yielding twelve kinds of fruit.

Trees of every kind,
And plants of every kind restored;
Every kind of animal will be returned.
The Garden of Eden is restored.

Land Of Harmony

In a beautiful land,
The lion and the lamb
Shall lie down side by side.

The bear and the calf,
In the meadows
Will play together in peace.

The leopard and the kid
Shall run together
And a little child shall lead them.

There is a beauty in the new earth;
And a beauty in the animals;
A beauty no words can ever describe.

In all its beauty,
A garden is restored;
A land where all live in harmony.

My Heavenly
Father's Heart

This is a collection of poems based mostly on scripture. It talks about creation and of Jesus birth, His life on this earth, His death and resurrection from death. It speaks of God's love and care for us and that He wants to be close to us and wants us in heaven with him. The poems speak of nature and how all nature praises God. They tell of what it will be like at the end of time. They also give and idea of what it will be like in heaven and when the new earth is created.

I was born and raised on a ranch in California. We had horses and hay crops. I learned to train horses from my father; and have shown them a few times

I now have a small place of my own with some horses that I ride for pleasure. I also work as a ranch hand on a horse ranch. My daughter has shown sheep and horses in 4-H and has done well with them. I grew up in a Christian family. I became a Christian when I was quite young. I learned to trust God more when I went through some hard times. God is always with me no matter what is going on in my life.